DATE DUE

JA 4 '93		
FE 18 '94		
DE 2 '94		
DE 2 2 '95		
MY 27 '97		
AP 29 '98		
JY 20 '99		
DE 13 '99		
AP 11 '00		
FE 8 '01		
MY 28 '02		

GREAT MYSTERIES

Life After Death

OPPOSING VIEWPOINTS®

Look for these and other exciting *Great Mysteries: Opposing Viewpoints* books:

GREAT MYSTERIES

Life After Death

OPPOSING VIEWPOINTS®

by Tom Schouweiler

Greenhaven Press, Inc.   P.O. Box 289009, San Diego, California 92128-9009

No part of this book may be reproduced or used in any form or by any means, electronic, mechanical, or otherwise, including but not limited to photocopy, recording, or any information storage, and retrieval system, without prior written permission from the publisher.

Library of Congress Cataloging-in-Publication Data

Schouweiler, Thomas, 1965-
    Life after death : opposing viewpoints / by
Thomas Schouweiler.
        p.   cm. — (Great mysteries)
    Includes bibliographical references and index.
    Summary: Explores the different viewpoints and
theories of existence after death, including reincarnation, heaven and hell, and annihilation.
    ISBN 0-89908-082-0
    1. Future life—Juvenile literature. [1. Future
life.] I. Title. II. Series: Great mysteries (Saint Paul,
Minn.)
BL535.S36   1990
133.9'C1'3—dc20   90-39092
                                                      CIP
                                                      AC

This book is dedicated
to the memory of
Francis Edward Schouweiler

"The boundaries which divide Life from Death are at best shadowy and vague. Who shall say where the one ends, and where the other begins?"

Edgar Allan Poe, "The Premature Burial"

Contents

Introduction

This book is written for the curious—those who want to explore the mysteries that are everywhere. To be human is to be constantly surrounded by wonderment. How do birds fly? Are ghosts real? Can animals and people communicate? Was King Arthur a real person or a myth? Why did Amelia Earhart disappear? Did history really happen the way we think it did? Where did the world come from? Where is it going?

Great Mysteries: Opposing Viewpoints books are intended to offer the reader an opportunity to explore some of the many mysteries that both trouble and intrigue us. For the span of each book, we want the reader to feel that he or she is a scientist investigating the extinction of the dinosaurs, an archaeologist searching for clues to the origin of the great Egyptian pyramids, a psychic detective testing the existence of ESP.

One thing all mysteries have in common is that there is no ready answer. Often there are *many* answers but none on which even the majority of authorities agrees. *Great Mysteries: Opposing Viewpoints* books introduce the intriguing views of the experts, allowing the reader to participate in their explorations, their theories, and their disagreements as they try to explain the mysteries of our world.

But most readers won't want to stop here. These *Great Mysteries: Opposing Viewpoints* aim to stimulate the reader's curiosity. Although truth is often impossible to discover, the search is fascinating. It is up to the reader to examine the evidence, to decide whether the answer is there—or to explore further.

"Penetrating so many secrets, we cease to believe in the unknowable. But there it sits nevertheless, calmly licking its chops."

H.L. Mencken, American essayist

One

Is There a Hereafter?

Human beings are curious by nature. In a world of differences, curiosity is one trait shared by all people. The history of the world was formed by people's desire to know what was previously unknown.

Curiosity led to the discovery of fire. Curiosity led Leif Eriksson and Christopher Columbus to sail westward and discover North and South America. Presumably, curiosity is why you are reading this book.

No matter how curious people are and how carefully they explore the world's puzzles, they cannot find the answers to every question. What happens after death is such a question. The answer has been sought through the centuries, yet it continues to be elusive.

Life After Death: A Hot Subject

What happens after death is something everybody wonders about. This is simply because all people come in contact with death when friends and loved ones die, and all know they

Opposite: What happens to us after we die? Monuments such as these are testimony to people's desire to be remembered. But do we live on in any other way?

The rituals of even the earliest people suggest that
they believed in some form of afterlife. This photo
shows the Smithsonian Museum of Natural History's
recreation of a 50,000-year-old burial found and
excavated in France. The deceased person was
bound with cords and placed in a pit lined with
bearskins and ritual offerings.

themselves will eventually die as well. Most human beings have difficulty believing life will come to an abrupt and final end. Most believe that there is some kind of existence after death. Scientists have found evidence that even prehistoric humans tried to prepare the dead for what lay ahead. For example, one hundred thousand years ago, Neanderthal humans placed food and flint tools in the graves with the bodies of their dead. Experts believe that the people thought the dead person would make use of these things in the world beyond. Many centuries later, between ten thousand and five thousand years ago, humans had developed complex funeral practices and built elaborate burial chambers. Belief in an afterlife had flourished. The idea of placing things in the burial chamber for use in the afterlife had gotten out of hand. In some cultures, including Egypt, wives and slaves were buried alive with powerful chieftains when they

Above: These are a few of the artifacts found in King Tut's tomb in Egypt in the 1920s. Left: The Egyptians were not alone in their elaborate preparations for the afterlife. This illustration shows an Incan burial in the early seventeenth century.

died! Clearly the idea of a continued existence after the death of the physical body was on the minds of ancient humans.

Continued existence, unending life, is called immortality. Not everyone believes in immortality, but most of the world's people believe in some form of afterlife. Each of the thousands of religions in the world has its own specific doctrines regarding the afterlife. Those who believe in no religion also have ideas about what happens after death.

A seventeenth-century tombstone from Salem, Massachusetts.

Many Different Ideas

Some people believe in paradise and punishment. These people believe that each person has one earthly life only. At the end of that life the person's spirit goes to a good place, such as heaven, or a bad place, such as hell. Generally, the stay at either place lasts forever.

Some people believe in reincarnation. Reincarnation is the belief that one spirit lives in many bodies throughout numerous earthly lifetimes. In other words, physical bodies last only one lifetime but the spirit moves into a new body when the old one "wears out" or dies. Reincarnationists believe that all of us have lived before — perhaps as sailors in the Viking navy, as midwives in ancient Greece, as Asian or South American mystics, or as farmers in Africa. And, say reincarnationists, we will live a different life when this one is over.

Some people believe that there is nothing after this life. They say that ideas like heaven or reincarnation are just wishful thinking because no one wants to die. All the evidence, they argue, indicates that nothing lies beyond the death of the body.

Among the billions of people in the world, many variations exist about these three ideas: spiritual life in heaven or hell; the cycle of life, death, and rebirth; and the end of existence. Which is the true one? The thoughtful person examines many ideas and draws his or her own conclusions.

"If I think of Death at all it is merely as a negation of life, a close, a last and necessary chord....My consciousness began in a very humble fashion with my body; with my body, very quietly, I hope it will end."

Archaeologist and author
Jane Harrison

"What is it to cease breathing, but to free the breath from its restless tides, that it may rise and expand and seek God unencumbered?"

Poet and philosopher
Kahlil Gibran

Two

Does Evidence Exist of Life After Death?

Opposite: Photographer
Duane Michels depicts an
out-of-body experience. Many
people who come close to
death have experiences like
this where their spirit seems
to leave their body behind. Is
this what dying is like?

Over the centuries, many philosophers have expressed a belief in life after death. Some have tried to prove it logically. But has anyone ever found firsthand evidence? Some people believe they have. Occasionally when people are seriously injured or very sick their hearts stop beating for a brief period of time, perhaps two or three minutes. In a way, they are dead for that time. Some of these people have near-death experiences, or NDEs. When they recover, they have a story to tell. They can describe what was happening around them while they were unconscious and their hearts were not beating. Often they can repeat the conversations of the doctors or relatives who were in the room with them.

But more important to the question of life after death, some of these people tell of a journey they took out of their bodies. No two stories have been identical, but almost all share common elements.

Amazing Stories

A psychiatrist named Raymond Moody has

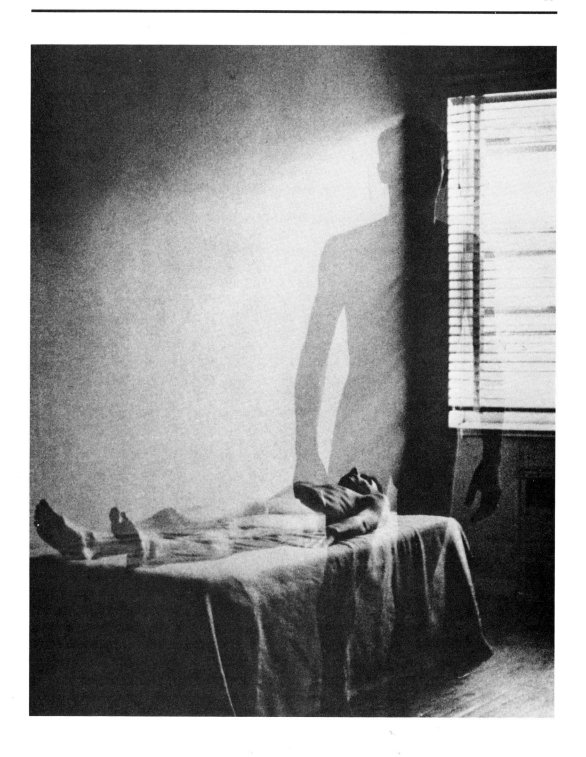

story 1

worked with people who were pronounced clinically dead and then were revived. He has published the testimony of these people in a book called *Life After Life*. Here is a part of a story told by one woman:

I found myself in a black void, and I knew that I had left my physical body behind. I knew I was dying...Immediately, I was moved out of that blackness, through a pale gray, and I just went on, gliding and moving swiftly...I could see a gray mist, and I was rushing toward it... Beyond the mist, I could see people, and their forms were just like they are on earth, and I could see...buildings. The whole thing was permeated with the most gorgeous light — a living, golden yellow...As I approached more closely, I felt certain that I was going through that mist. It was such a wonderful, joyous feeling...It wasn't my time to go through the mist, because instantly from the other side appeared my uncle Carl, who had died many years earlier. He blocked my path, saying, "Go back. Your work on earth has not been completed. Go back now." I didn't want to

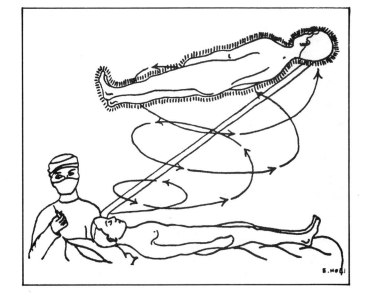

This illustration shows the experience of a Dutch school caretaker who was badly injured in an accident. During surgery for his injuries he had a near-death experience.

go back, but I had no choice, and immediately I was back in my body. I felt that horrible pain in my chest, and I heard my little boy crying "...Bring my mommy back to me!"

Here is testimony from another person Dr. Moody interviewed. Notice how similar the two stories are.

[I heard my doctor say that] I wasn't going to make it. He told my relatives to come because I wasn't going to be here much longer. They came and gathered around my bed. My relatives looked like they were going farther and farther away from me. It got dimmer and dimmer but I saw them. ...[The next thing I knew] I was in a narrow, V-shaped passage...It just fit my body, and my hands and arms seemed to be down at my side. I went head first, and it was dark, dark as it could be in there. I moved on through it...and I looked up and saw a beautiful polished door with no knob. Around the edges of the door I could see a really brilliant light...[It seemed like] everybody was so happy in there...It seemed awfully busy in there.

Notice the similarities in these two recollections: the darkness, the feeling of moving through a tunnel, the bright light, and the crowds of happy people.

Stages of a Near-Death Experience

Dr. Moody has arrived at a general outline of what happens during a near-death experience. He arrived at this conclusion by comparing all the available stories of NDEs.

First there is an overwhelming feeling of peace and a sense of well-being. This is especially remarkable because many of the people were in states of great pain when they "died."

The second stage is separating from the body and leaving it behind. Some people noted that they looked back and saw their bodies. A man

"In a surprisingly large percentage of patients who undergo a close call with death there occurs a transcendent... experience."

Near-death experience researcher Dr. Raymond Moody

"The simple imagery of the visions—tunnels, lights, and colors—are probably caused by a discharge of neurons in the eye."

Psychologist Ronald Siegel

The fifteenth-century Dutch artist Hieronymus Bosch often painted scenes of heaven and hell. This portion of "Ascent into the Empyrium" depicts something similar to what many people say they experience in an NDE: traveling through a tunnel into light where other-worldly beings often await.

who was badly injured in a car crash told Dr. Moody: "At that time I viewed myself from the corner of the hospital room, looking down at my body which was very dark and gray. All the life looked like it was out of it."

In the next stage, the person enters darkness. Often this darkness takes the form of a trough or tunnel, as in the second example. People have told Dr. Moody that the blackness was total but that they were not afraid of it. Most people felt that they were moving through the blackness at a high speed.

After leaving the darkness, the people entered a bright light. Though the light was intense, people reported that it did not hurt their eyes. They said that the light was comforting and beautiful. One woman recalls thinking, "That's a funny light. It doesn't even look like gold yet it is gold

Patterns of NDEs

Most NDEs seem to be pleasant experiences. Some people feel as though they travel through beautiful, peaceful scenery with meadows, flowers, and lakes.

Some NDEs are not pleasant. One man was confronted with snarling beasts. What is the meaning of these experiences?

and it isn't yellow." The movement out of the body, through the darkness, and into light is a consistent pattern found in NDEs.

Different Endings

Some experiences end with the light. A few people report seeing people, places, and amazing things inside the light. One man who spoke with Dr. Moody recalled:

> I saw the most beautiful lakes. Everything was white. The most beautiful flowers. Nobody on this earth ever saw the beautiful flowers I saw there...I don't believe there is a color on this earth that wasn't in that color situation I saw... Everything was bright. The lakes were blue, light blue.

A woman who almost died from a cerebral hemorrhage described a lane in "a beautiful meadow."

Not everyone who describes near-death experiences describes those scenes of beautiful meadows and flowers. Kenneth Ring is a psychologist who also studies near-death experiences. In Ring's book *Life at Death*, a man who was dangerously ill from blood poisoning related this experience:

> I was alone. On an endless expanse of plain. Dry brown grass up on the distant horizon. All over it a pale sky with racing clouds. Then they came over the last hills. Yellow wolves in a solid front. Wave upon wave, rippling backs, noisily advancing...on me!...The beasts...foaming at the mouth, teeth bared. Close ranked, facing me. I gripped, in mounting fear, with both hands. But I grasped only air...over and over again.

The fact that this last story is so different from the other accounts reminds us that we do not know what to make of all these experiences. Drs. Moody and Ring suggest they are a glimpse of what awaits us for all eternity. Will the woman who saw the country meadow lane go to heaven? Will the man who saw the wolves go to hell? Some people think NDEs show a sort of otherworldly waiting room, a place to go while waiting to go to the final afterlife destination. Perhaps that destination is heaven or hell; perhaps it is another

Do NDEs show that when we die, our spirits go to an "otherworldly waiting room" before going on to a more permanent place? This scene from the movie *Beetlejuice* shows a comic and strange waiting room in the afterlife.

Some experts say that NDEs have nothing to do with the real experience of dying. They point out that similar experiences happen when a person is under the influence of drugs. This scene from the movie *Altered States* shows a man undergoing a strange out-of-body experience.

life on earth.

The accounts of peaceful meadows, beautiful music, and an overwhelming feeling of contentment are appealing. Most people want to believe death is not final, that there is some kind of afterlife. However, the possibility that these stories say nothing about life after death must also be considered.

Other Explanations for NDEs

Even Dr. Moody admits that his work cannot prove anything about life after death because none of the people he spoke with actually died. He states, "Obviously...none of my cases would qualify [as proof of life after death,] since they all involved resuscitation."

It is important to keep this in mind when considering the work of Dr. Moody and all NDE stories. The people interviewed cannot claim to

describe what *death* is like, but rather what *dying* is like. There is a difference between the two. Moody believes that NDEs are a preview of life after death. Other people have more mundane explanations.

Hans Küng is a Catholic theologian, a specialist in religious belief. He points out that there are scientific or medical explanations for near-death experiences. He says that the kinds of things observed during NDEs can also be seen independently of the process of dying. For instance, a bright light is sometimes seen by people under the influence of mind-altering drugs.

Robert Siegel, a psychologist at the University of California, notes that some of the things described in NDE stories are strikingly similar to experiences during drug-induced hallucinations and hallucinations produced by other means. A

Some experts believe that the tunnel and the light commonly experienced during an NDE are the result of cultural conditioning. People learn that God is light and so, when the mind is in an altered state because of a traumatic experience such as nearly dying, the mind sees what it expects to see.

Artist Amy Johnson depicts a common circumstance
for an NDE.

hallucination is when somebody sees things, hears things, or touches things that are not actually there. The bright light, the tunnel experience, the separation from the body, the floating feeling, and the encounter with familiar figures are often elements of hallucinations. Siegel speculates that the physical process of dying may bring them about.

Dr. Siegel says NDE visions may be a defense reaction caused by fear of death. The dying person may be so afraid of death that the brain escapes the fearful situation by creating a dreamland. The brain calls up all the information it has learned about death and memories of the past. Since American people commonly associate God with light, that is what a person's brain creates as it dies. The brain creates an acceptable scheme for its own death. It remembers everything learned about dying, such as what heaven is supposed to be like, that God is associated with light, and that the spirit is supposed to separate from the body. Death is less frightening because it is more familiar. Since most Americans learn similar things about death, they create similar images for themselves.

Profound Experience

Whatever they are, NDEs have a profound affect upon the lives of people who experience them. Dr. Moody reports that people who have NDEs are no longer afraid to die and often approach life with a renewed sense of purpose. Perhaps NDEs are the creation of frightened minds. It is also possible that they are a vision of what happens immediately after death.

If that is the case, then what comes after the light that people see in near-death experiences? Do they stay with the light? Or do they move on to heaven, hell, or rebirth?

"Research such as Dr. Moody presents in his book...will enlighten many and will confirm what we have been taught for two thousand years—that there is life after death."

Psychologist Elizabeth Kübler-Ross

"NDE accounts are definitely and strongly influenced by culture.... They are not simply literal accounts of the afterlife. Indeed, they are shot through with elements from this life."

Rodney Clapp, associate editor of *Christianity Today*

Three

Do People Go to Heaven and Hell?

In 1982, the Gallup organization asked Americans about their beliefs concerning life after death. The poll showed that 71 percent of Americans think there is a heaven. Heaven is seen as a place where people go after they die if they have led good lives. There they will be eternally rewarded. Five percent of the people surveyed believed eternity in heaven would be boring. Hell is defined as a place people who have led bad lives go to be punished forever.

Another poll, this time of American Catholics, was conducted by *U.S. Catholic* magazine. It found that most Catholic people believe that after death they will be able to interact with God and meet dead family members, even "our first baby who died and that I have never seen." The people surveyed had different ideas about heaven. One viewed it as an isolated spot in the country; another visualized it as a place filled with whatever pleases each individual; and one person thought heaven would be the kind of place where lots of baseball would be played.

Christians and Jews call their version of the

heaven or hell

afterlife paradise *heaven*, and their version of the afterlife punishment *hell*. Because North American culture is chiefly Judeo-Christian, heaven and hell are probably the most familiar names when we think of eternal afterlife. But many other cultures also believe that there are good and bad places, with different names, where people go when they die. Though each culture's version of paradise is different, there are some basic assumptions that are shared by most people who believe in eternal reward or punishment for everyone.

People who believe in eternal punishment and reward believe that each person has only one life on earth. At the end of that life, the person goes to one of the two places and stays there for all eternity. The way a person conducts his or her life determines which place he or she goes to.

Sheol

A long time ago, heaven and hell were not clearly differentiated. There was no idea of reward or punishment. The afterlife was a mysterious undefined place. The ancient Hebrews first wrote about it around 700 B.C. They called it *Sheol*.

Sheol was a huge underground pit where the dead went. This may have been a magnified version of a tribal burial pit, according to David Hick, author of *Death and Eternal Life*. Hick has studied beliefs of the afterlife throughout history. He theorizes that the ancients may have taken an idea they were sure of — the burial pit — and expanded upon it in order to picture what happened to the dead.

In the Bible, Job calls Sheol "the land of gloom and deep darkness, the land of gloom and chaos, where light is as darkness." Sheol was a permanent residence for the dead. Job said that

Archaeologist Leon Fort is supervising the excavation of a burial pit in France believed to be from the Stone Age. Some anthropologists believe burial sites like this inspired Sheol, the early Hebrew idea of afterlife.

"he who goes down to Sheol does not come up."

Current Jewish, Muslim, and Christian ideas of the afterlife are based on the concept of Sheol. Each religion borrowed the concept and changed it in a different way.

Elysian Fields and Amenti

The idea of judgment of the dead and eternal reward or punishment was first recorded more than four thousand years ago in ancient Egypt. The Egyptian idea of the afterlife contains the three essential elements of modern Judeo-Christian doctrine: judgment, heaven, and hell. Later Egyptians called heaven the *Elysian Fields* and hell *Amenti*.

To an ancient Egyptian, the judgment after death was a long and intricate process with many participants. The newly dead person was taken by

Ancient Egyptians believed that part of the final judgment was the weighing of the person's heart to determine his or her worthiness. This papyrus painting shows some of the Egyptian gods and the scale on which the heart was weighed.

celestial (heavenly) attendants to Osiris, the god in charge of the afterlife, and a group of lesser gods. The next step was a confession in which the person went through a list of sins, denying them all. For example, the dead person would say, "I have not pried into matters to make mischief," or "I have not uttered curses against the pharoah."

After the dead person was finished, his or her heart was weighed on a divine scale to determine the truthfulness of the confession. If the dead person passed, then came the last test, recognizing and naming all the lesser gods — and there were a lot of them! If this was accomplished, then the dead person could go to the Elysian Fields. Failure to pass the test resulted in a trip to Amenti.

Amenti is the first mention of a truly horrible punishment for the dead. In the book *Egyptian Ideas of the Future Life*, E. A. Wallis quotes from an ancient Egyptian holy man's description of Amenti. The holy man said, "In Amenti...[there are] pits and ditches filled with fire, and other [people] are in the river of fire." He related a tale told to him by a man who had claimed to have gone to Amenti and returned. The man described "tormentors who were without pity and who each had a different form." These "wild beasts...inflicted punishment upon" him and led the man to

a great ditch...filled with reptiles; each reptile had seven heads and the body of each was like...a scorpion. [There was also] the Great Worm, the mere sight of which terrified [whoever saw it]. In his mouth he had teeth like...iron stakes, and one [of the beasts] took me and threw me to this Worm which never ceased to eat; then immediately all the beasts gathered together near him and when he had filled his mouth [with my

The Egyptian hell, Amenti, was said to have a Great Worm that tormented those who were sent there. Gustave Doré, in an illustration from Italian poet Dante Alghieri's twelfth-century masterpiece, *Purgatorio*, also shows suffering souls in the clutches of "Great Worms."

Egypt Hell

Egypt Heaven

Hindu Heaven

flesh], all the beasts who were round about me filled theirs.

Note that both this and the Judeo-Christian version of hell involved unrelenting torture, fire, and demons.

The Elysian Fields, however, were not much like Judeo-Christian concepts of heaven. The Elysian Fields were not a blissful spiritual realm. They were a compilation and exaggeration of all that was best in earthly life for the ancient Egyptian. In fact, the Elysian Fields were thought of as a distant place on earth rather than a place in the sky or another dimension. The Elysian Fields had no snow, rain, extreme heat, or harsh winds. Instead there was always a cool, pleasant breeze.

It was a fertile place where land could be farmed easily and with high yields. There were many canals for irrigating crops. It was a place where everyone could have a well-stocked household and leisure time to enjoy these advantages.

Egypt was (and is) a hot, dry place where farming was difficult and frequently unrewarding. It makes sense that an Egyptian's idea of heaven would be a place where farming was easy and much food could be obtained from it. Here we see that a concrete idea — agriculture — was the basis for a concept of the afterlife, the Elysian Fields.

Ancient Hindu

Like the Egyptians, the ancient people of India drew their concept of paradise from the real pleasures of earth. Three thousand years ago Indians thought of heaven as a spacious hall and a garden. In the garden were beautiful trees and flowers, good food, and flowing streams of milk and honey. This heaven was an exclusive one. It was reserved only for those who were rigorously religious, for war heroes, and above all for those who offered generous sacrificial gifts to the gods.

The Hindus viewed the afterlife paradise as a lush
place filled with flowers, fruits, peace, and luxury.

Much was written about hell by the ancient Hindus. Hell was separated into 136 compartments, each designed to punish a specific sin. In *Heaven and Hell in Comparative Religion*, religious scholar Dr. Kaufmann Kohler describes the various tortures. "The eyes of the lustful or the envious were pulled out by the sharp beaks of birds." The liar's tongue was "hacked to pieces by pointed swords." Hands and feet used in any evil act were dunked into a cauldron of boiling liquid.

Hindu Hell

Ancient Hindus gathered information about heaven and hell from legends about kings and saints who died temporarily and experienced the afterlife. In one such legend a very fair and merciful king achieved a wonderful existence in heaven but was later sent to hell because of his unkind treatment of his domestic animals on earth. The king saw mud, blood, and flames in hell. Vultures feasted on the flesh of human victims. In the legend, the king disregarded his own pain and had sympathy for the inhabitants of hell. In so doing, he brought relief to those people, and his unselfish act made it possible for him to return to heaven.

To ancient Indians, as to ancient Egyptians, life in heaven was an easier and happier version of life on earth. Hell was a place of unending physical torture. Some tribes of African natives also have similar ideas about the hereafter.

African Beliefs

Africa is a huge continent comprised of a large number of tribes, many of whom are isolated from each other. Each tribe's beliefs are different, although many share similarities. These ideas stretch back thousands of years and continue today. Tokundo Adeyemo, an African and an expert in African religious belief, discusses these

Opposite page: People of many cultures believed that the afterlife included distinct punishments for different kinds of sins. This fifteenth-century French woodcut shows a punishment for Greed, one of the seven deadly sins. The greedy are put into cauldrons of boiling oil. Below: A sixteenth-century German woodcut depicting hell.

The Bachwa tribe of Zaire, Africa, believe the soul is located in the pupil of the eye.

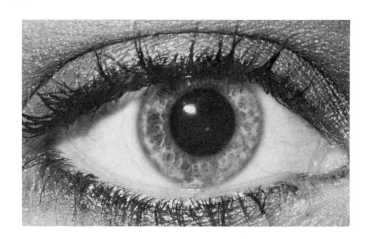

beliefs in his book *Salvation in African Tradition*.

The Bachwa tribe of Zaire believe that the soul is located in the pupil of the eye. At death, the eye breaks, the soul leaves, and the body ceases to function. The Chagga of Tanzania believe that when the soul departs it begins an eight-day journey across the desert. On the ninth day, it arrives at the world of the afterlife.

Some African peoples believe that the afterlife is located underground. The Bambuti of Zaire call it "the kingdom of the dead." The Akamba of Kenya believe the afterlife is located in the woods, in solitary rocks, and in natural pools of water.

In the jungle nation of Angola, the Bacongo tribe believe the dead live in a spirit village in a great mysterious forest. The Bamileke of Cameroon believe that each dead person inhabits his or her former skull. According to the Ga tribe of Ghana, the dead "linger around their former homes for forty years, and move on after that." Many African tribes feel that the dead go to a place that is much like the earth. Social and political status is maintained there. Wealth or poverty is reproduced. Human activities continue.

Other African tribal beliefs resemble Judeo-Christian ones in the traditions of judgment, heaven, and hell. For example, the Yoruba tribe of Nigeria fear judgment in the afterlife. At death, they believe, the soul leaves the body and travels to God, or *Olodumare*. There the deceased is asked to give an account of how his or her earthly life was spent. Olodumare and his deputy, Obatala, evaluate the character of the dead person. The individual is then sent to either heaven or hell. The stay at either place lasts forever.

Hell is a place of suffering and punishment for the wicked. Heaven is a pleasant place very similar to the earth. There the deceased is greeted by rejoicing dead relatives and associates. There are none of the toils or sorrows associated with earthly life.

These views are very similar to those found in ancient India and Egypt. These ideas are also similar to those of Native Americans.

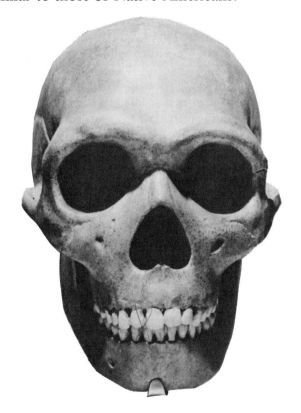

The Bamileke tribe of Cameroon, Africa, believe each dead person inhabits his or her former skull.

Native American Beliefs

Many native North Americans, or American Indians, were noted for living in harmony with nature. Historically, most did not build cities, and they were not interested in developing technology. Instead, they chose to live in close connection with nature. Their ideas about heaven reflected this lifestyle.

Like the ancient Egyptians and the Bacongo and other tribes in Africa, certain Native Americans believed that the afterlife was a physical spot on earth located a great distance away. Ellen R. Robinson studied the afterlife beliefs of Native Americans. In her book *Indian Myths*, she tells the Algonquin tribe's legend of the young chief whose wife died on the eve of their marriage. The young chief was so sad about this that he set out for the Land of Souls. The only thing he knew about this place was that it was south, so he traveled south. Snow was on the ground when he left. As he traveled, the surrounding woods became more cheerful in appearance; there were leaves on the trees, flowers on the ground, and a clear sky. The young chief took these things as a sign that he was on the right path.

Eventually he reached a cabin. An old man was there. The old man pointed out beyond the cabin. He said, "It is the Land of Souls. You stand upon its borders...but you cannot take your body with you. Leave it here. You will find it safe upon your return."

The young chief soon found that he was able to fly. He also noticed that things were more colorful and beautiful. The birds were more exotic than he was used to. The water was clearer and the plants more lush. The young chief could walk right through the trees. He deduced that they must be the souls of trees. They had left their bodies behind just as he had.

He came to a large lake that had an island in the middle. The young chief saw a white canoe on the shore. He got into the canoe and crossed to the island.

The island seemed a blissful place to him. There were no storms and no cold. There was plenty to eat and no one died. There was no war and no hunting. He saw his dead wife.

Eventually, he was instructed to return to the Land of the Living because it was not yet his time. He rejoined his body and went back to his tribe.

This is another example in which the concept of the afterlife derived from circumstances of everyday life. The closeness that Native Americans felt with nature can be seen in the fact that even the trees in this story went to heaven.

In all the above examples, the various conceptions of heaven and hell are based on concrete,

The American Indian Algonquin tribe tells a traditional story of a young chief who travels to the afterlife to visit his dead wife.

In medieval Europe, Heaven was viewed as being like a busy city. This illustration is taken from a fifteenth-century French edition of St. Augustine's *The City of God.*

everyday things. Over time these basic concepts were expanded upon and changed. A good example of this is the changes that occurred a few centuries ago in European Christian ideas about heaven.

Christian Heavens

The European medieval period, or Middle Ages, lasted from 476 A.D. to around 1450 A.D. Unlike today, society then changed very slowly. Colleen McDannell and Bernhard Lang studied how the Christian view of heaven has changed over time. They published the results in a book called *Heaven: A History*.

During the Middle Ages, the most popular image of heaven was a city. This image can be found in the Bible, where the city is called New Jerusalem. It was a magnificent place with streets made from the purest gold and precious stones. Alongside each street were golden trees. All the surroundings were said to be more glorious than could be imagined. New Jerusalem was composed of seven separate castles connected by lush and luxurious gardens. All of the castles were visited three times yearly by Jesus Christ, the Virgin Mary, angels, archangels, apostles, prophets, and saints.

This image contrasted with the reality of city life in the Middle Ages. Cities had narrow streets and their inhabitants dressed in coarse clothing. Castles were cold and drafty. Perhaps this is why the city of heaven was a hospitable, warm, and inviting place.

Then came the Renaissance. It started around 1400 and lasted until 1600. Renaissance means "rebirth," and that is what happened in Europe during this time. There was a great revival of art, literature, and learning during the Renaissance. Old ideas about life were re-thought and modified or thrown out.

"Life is eternal; Death is merely a change in conditions."

Levi Smith, a founder of the Church of Latter Day Saints

"The immortality myth... is no longer relevant to human concerns."

Paul Kurtz, *In Defense of Secular Humanism*

The perception of heaven changed. During the Renaissance, heaven was seen as a pastoral, or natural, place very much like the Garden of Eden. The garden of heaven had trees, flowers, and meadows, but did not contain dangerous animals or plants. Besides the garden, there was also a large temple in heaven. Inhabitants could move between the temple and the countryside, going to the temple only to worship.

Renaissance ideas about the activities of the inhabitants of heaven were considerably more relaxed than those of the Middle Ages. Renaissance people believed that the dead in heaven played, touched, danced, listened to music, and generally passed eternity in pleasure. The inhabitants wore no clothes. Heaven had no social classes; anyone could interact with anyone else. In keeping with the general attitude of the Renaissance, the emphasis was on love rather than worship.

This comparison shows that the ideas of heaven over time vary as much as the conceptions of heaven between various religions. The two examples above are as different as the city and the country. What was happening in the culture of a society affected its vision of what paradise would be like.

Today there are many different Christian sects and many of them have distinctive views of what heaven and hell will be like. Some have vague ideas; some have very specific ideas. The most specific images of heaven can be found in the writings of the Church of the Latter Day Saints, otherwise known as the Mormons.

The Church of the Latter Day Saints

Mormons believe that hell is a place where the wicked person's bad qualities are magnified. This person must live with other people who are similar in character. Therefore, hell is rife with guilt,

This nineteenth-century illustration depicts "Summerland," a place not quite heaven and not quite earth, where good souls were believed to go to become nearer God. Its pastoral environment resembles the ideas of Renaissance Europe about heaven.

Europeans of the Renaissance period believed heaven
was a merry place filled with earthly pleasures.

fear, lust, rage, and spite.

Heaven, on the other hand, is a beautiful place containing lakes, forests, brilliant flowers, and remarkable buildings. People know each other and are friendly. Spirits act with the abilities they had or would have had in their earthly primes. The child who died at birth can be the adult he would have been, and the old woman can be the vigorous young woman she once was.

Unlike most other ideas of heaven, the Mormon heaven is a busy place. That is because work is so important to Mormons. Mormon leaders are busy teaching, doing missionary work, and guiding new entrants into heaven. Work continues there.

Even though babies become adults in heaven, they can be babies if they need to be. In fact, Mary Hill, a Mormon theologian, claims that a person who dies in infancy becomes an adult in heaven but reverts back to the child state when his or her mother dies. This happens so that the mother can enjoy caring for her child, which she missed in her life on earth. Hill arrived at this conclusion after careful study of Mormon doctrine and her own unusual experience after losing a child.

McDannell and Lang relate the story she told. Hill was sad that her fifth child, Stephen, had died even though she believed that he was in heaven. She became especially anxious when her next child was about to be born, fearing that child would die young as well.

After the birth of her sixth child, Mary Hill lay in the recovery room, and she believed she saw Stephen. "His hair was sandy colored with a soft wave in it, and his jaw square and muscular," she remembers. Stephen told her, "Well, Mother, now you have your baby, and there's no more need to grieve for me. We'll have our time in the

Mormon Mary Hill had a personal experience that convinced her that families are reunited in the afterlife.

The family is extremely important to Mormons. They believe that family members will be together for eternity after death. This painting depicts "An Eternal Family."

resurrection, and now I'm free to do my work in the spirit world."

Family life is very important in Mormon belief. Child-bearing is even possible in heaven for couples who go through a special marriage ceremony on earth, and who are Mormons in good standing. A part of most marriage ceremonies are the words "til death do you part." Certain Mormons are permitted to be married not only for the extent of their lives on earth, but for all eternity as well!

The Mormons believe that such couples continue after death to have "spirit children." These children who are born in heaven are spiritual in nature, rather than human babies. These spirit people travel to different planets where they inhabit physical bodies. Their parents are to that planet as God is to the earth. "Just as [people] were first born as spirit children to their Eternal Father and...Queen Mother, the children born to resurrected beings are spirit beings and must be sent...to another earth to pass through the trials of mortality and obtain a physical body," said Diane Crowther, a Mormon thinker.

An etching from "The Grave," a long poem by eighteenth-century poet, artist, and mystic William Blake. This illustration shows a family reunited in heaven.

The idea of spirit children is unique to the Mormons. Each different religion has different ideas and elements in their beliefs about the afterlife. The Catholic church is another significant Christian religion. One element unique to Catholicism is a belief in purgatory.

Purgatory

Purgatory is an afterlife that is not quite hell, and not heaven either. It is a place of temporary punishment. In the Middle Ages, there was a debate among Catholic theologians about what happened to people who did not deserve to go instantly to heaven but did not deserve to suffer in hell forever.

In purgatory the deceased would be punished for sins committed while alive. When those sins were made up for, that person would then be allowed to go on to heaven for the rest of eternity. In the sixth century, Gregory the Great, a Catholic leader, made purgatory part of Catholic doctrine even though it has no basis in biblical writing.

In *Heaven and Hell in Comparative Literature*, Dr. Kohler talks about a monk named Alberic who lived in the twelfth century. His vision of purgatory became the accepted one in the Catholic church at that time. In his purgatory, some people were punished by alternating fire and ice. Others were hung up by the body part with which they had sinned. Even more severe punishments were inflicted on those who had been more evil.

At the boundary of purgatory was a river of fire with an iron bridge over it. This bridge was easy to pass for those who had received enough punishment to be purified of their sins, but for those who remained wicked it became increasingly narrow until they fell off into the river of fire. After the bridge was a road covered with thorns.

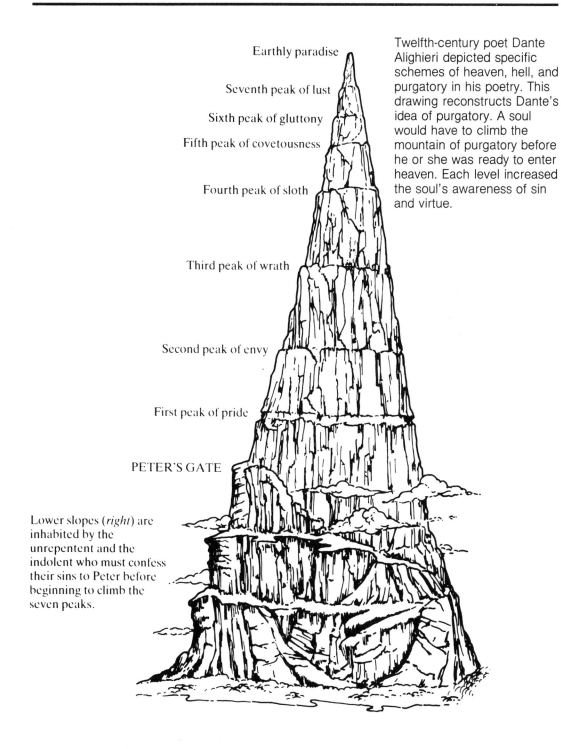

Earthly paradise

Seventh peak of lust

Sixth peak of gluttony

Fifth peak of covetousness

Fourth peak of sloth

Third peak of wrath

Second peak of envy

First peak of pride

PETER'S GATE

Lower slopes (*right*) are inhabited by the unrepentent and the indolent who must confess their sins to Peter before beginning to climb the seven peaks.

Twelfth-century poet Dante Alighieri depicted specific schemes of heaven, hell, and purgatory in his poetry. This drawing reconstructs Dante's idea of purgatory. A soul would have to climb the mountain of purgatory before he or she was ready to enter heaven. Each level increased the soul's awareness of sin and virtue.

One idea of purgatory is that it is a bridge between heaven and hell. After undergoing sufficient punishment to make up for sins committed, a purified soul could pass over the bridge to get into heaven.

After traveling the road, the deceased was given the final test of purification, and then that person passed into heaven.

Today, such a terrifying vision of purgatory is widely considered to be out of date. Some now define purgatory as an absence of God. Others see it as a waiting room for heaven. The question of what purgatory is like — and whether it exists at all — continues to be discussed among Catholic thinkers. Most Catholics do continue to believe there is a middle ground for those not good enough to go immediately to heaven, but not deserving of eternal punishment either.

Hell

Like heaven, the Christian idea of hell emerged from the ancient hebrew concept of Sheol. Sheol means "the underworld" and is based on the concept of a mass grave.

As the idea of heaven as a reward for the good arose, so did the idea of hell as punishment for the bad. The Hebrews called it *Gehenna*.

Gehenna was a place where the deceased were burned by endless flames. This idea was based on a reality. According to novelist and theologian Harry Blamires in his book *Knowing the Truth About Heaven and Hell*, Gehenna was originally a valley located southwest of Jerusalem. This valley was used by people who worshipped idols and sacrificed other humans. About twenty-five hundred years ago, King Josea put a stop to these practices and turned the valley of Gehenna into a garbage-burning area. Because of Gehenna's connections with suffering, with cruel and non-Hebrew religious practices, and with fire, the word *Gehenna* became associated with the idea of eternal fiery punishment and separation from God.

By the second century A.D., early Christians had elaborated on the ancient concept of hell but

Hell is often depicted as fiery. Here, Gustave Doré, in an illustration from Dante's *Visions of Hell*, depicts the lost souls caught for eternity in a rain of fire.

changed it very little. As with purgatory, each sin had a particular punishment. In *The Devil's Dominion*, Anthony Masters described some of these punishments: People who had spoken disrespectfully about God were hung over fire by their tongues. Selfish rich people were continually rolled over sharp stones.

Unlike heaven, the idea of hell was not developed primarily by religious leaders. Poets and writers have supplied the most memorable visions of hell.

In the early twentieth-century novel *Portrait of the Artist as a Young Man*, Irish writer James Joyce has one of his characters, a Jesuit priest, describe hell in a sermon. It is a gruesome extension of the hell imagined by early Christians. The priest depicts the damned imprisoned under walls four thousand miles thick. He says bodies are heaped and crushed together so that an individual cannot move his arm to brush away the worm that gnaws at his eye. All the world's sewage and filth and dirt runs into hell. Adding to the horrible stench is the smell of burning bodies and rotting flesh. In Joyce's hell, the punishment is clearly torture inflicted by the devil.

Christopher Marlowe was a playwright in England during the sixteenth century. His most famous play is *Dr. Faustus*. In it, Dr. Faustus sells his soul to the devil in return for restoration to youth. Dr. Faustus asks the devil why he is not in hell. The devil replies that for him, the earth is hell:

> Why this is hell, nor am I out of it
> Thinkest thou that I, who saw the face of God
> And tasted the eternal joys of heaven,
> Am not tormented with ten thousand hells
> In being deprived of everlasting bliss?

In other words, for the devil in *Dr. Faustus* the punishment of hell is not physical torture; it is

Opposite page: Another view of hell in which people are tormented during all eternity for the sins they committed while alive. Below: Today, many theologians believe hell is not physical punishment but separation from God for all eternity.

separation from God. Though Joyce lived four hundred years after Marlowe, Marlowe's idea of hell being separation from God is closer to the concept of hell accepted by most modern biblical scholars. This separation, they maintain, would be as unpleasant as eternal torture.

Judaism

The Judaic, or Jewish, conception of heaven and hell is very similar to Christian ideas. Christianity, after all, grew out of Judaism. Therefore, both Christianity and Judaism share the concept of Sheol as a common origin for the belief in the afterlife.

A very important element in Jewish thought is resurrection. Rather than dying and going directly to heaven or hell, Jews believe that the dead stay dead for a while. They stay in a sort of limbo, a waiting place that is neither hell nor heaven, until "the end of time." At the end of time the messiah will come, the dead will be resurrected, and there will be a judgment of everyone.

The Torah, holy book of the Jews, says: "Many of those that sleep in the dust of the earth shall awake, some to everlasting life and some to shame and everlasting contempt." Those that "sleep in the dust" are the dead who will be resurrected or "awakened" and will then be judged either worthy of "everlasting life" or "everlasting shame," heaven or hell.

The Jewish view of heaven is similar to a temple, because spirituality and learning are emphasized. Heaven is not a physical place as it is for the Mormons. The Torah says, "Nothing occurs in the world to come which would involve bodies, such as sitting and standing, sleep and death, sadness and laughter.... There is no eating, drinking, or sexual intercourse in the world to come." In other words, it is a realm of the spirit only.

As in Mormon thought, there is an emphasis

on continued learning in heaven. The dead in heaven have access to knowledge unattainable on earth. According to the Torah, "They know and derive from the Truth of the Holy One...what they do not know in this world, confined by a dull and lowly body."

The Judaic heaven is a cumulation of everything regarded as good: "life unaccompanied by death, good unaccompanied by evil." Hell, on the other hand, is nothing at all. In Judaism annihilation is regarded as equivalent to hell. "The punishment of the wicked," states the Torah, "is that they will not merit such life but will be utterly cut off in their death. [This person] is cut off in his wickedness and perishes like an animal." Because life itself is so important in Jewish thought, annihilation is seen as a greater punishment than eternal torture.

Islam

Islam is the religion of many of the people of

Most ideas of what an afterlife is like come from the holy scriptures of various religions. Left, a man holds a scroll from the Jewish Torah. Right, a man holds an Islamic Koran.

Jewish - TORAH   Islamic - Koran

Many different religions believe that there will be a Last Judgment. On that day, people will be called from their graves or from the afterlife they are experiencing and will be given a final afterlife assignment.

Saudi Arabia, Iran, Iraq, and much of Northern Africa. Islam is similar to Judaism and Christianity in its doctrines of heaven and hell. Islam, Judaism, and Christianity share much common history. The sacred writings of all three of these religions contain stories of Noah, Abraham, David, Moses, and Jesus.

Muslims, those who profess the Islamic faith, call God *Allah*, the Arabic word for "Supreme Being of the Muslims." Though Muslims are interested in the words of Moses and Jesus, they believe Mohammed was the true messenger of Allah.

Mohammed lived from 570 to 632 A.D. He wrote the Koran, the holy book of Islam. Muslims believe that Allah spoke and Mohammed wrote down what Allah said.

Islam is similar to Judaism and Christianity in its views toward death and immortality. After death is a judgment and paradise for the good and hell for the bad. Muslims believe there will be resurrection and another judgment at the end of an unspecified time period.

At the time of death, according to Muslim belief, an angel appears to the recently deceased. The angel asks three important questions: Who is your lord, what is your religion, and who is your prophet? The correct answers are, of course, Allah, Islam, and Mohammed. If these answers are given, the angels send the newly deceased person on to paradise. If an unsatisfactory answer is given, two angels beat the deceased between the eyes and that person is sent on to hell.

Hell is a place of fire, extreme heat, and no water. Angels of Allah punish the damned. They show no mercy. When the inhabitants of hell cry out for water, "they will be served dream water like molten copper that will scald their entire being," according to Lex Hixon. He is the author of

Heart of the Koran, a book of studies on the Koran.

The Muslim paradise is a place of physical and spiritual pleasure. It is a luxurious environment. There is food and wine. It is a "garden with rivers of pure water, milk and honey," says Hixon. People are dressed in the finest clothing and wear gold jewelry. There is also spiritual satisfaction and much time is devoted to worship. The best element of paradise for Muslims is the opportunity to see the face of Allah.

The time of the resurrection is known only to Allah, but it will be signaled on earth by the blowing of a trumpet. This sound will strike fear into the hearts of all people. Buildings and mountains will be leveled; the sun will be blotted out. The oceans and seas and lakes will dry up.

There will then be a second blast of the trumpet. At that time, souls of the dead will rejoin their bodies and all people will go to an assembly place for the final judgment. Each person will be handed a record of his or her good and

Angel from a sixteenth-century Islamic painting.

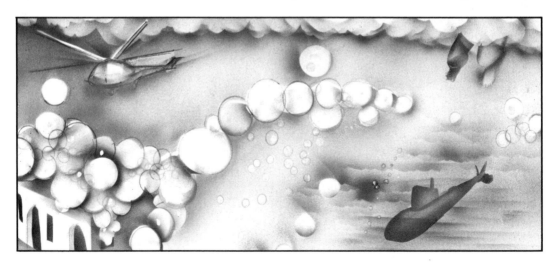

bad deeds and will be asked to read it. Everyone will then walk a bridge that passes through hell to paradise. Those who were good pass through quickly and receive very little punishment. Those who were bad or did not believe in Islam stay in hell forever.

Another Modern Conception of Heaven

Some concepts of the afterlife are based not on religious ideas but on human psychology. One such idea is suggested by H. H. Price, who was a professor at Oxford University. Price uses dreams as a model for both heaven and hell. He does this for two reasons: first, because a dream is something everybody experiences and knows is real; second, because the dream state involves the mind and not the body. Because the body is gone after death, Price feels that a dream is the best model available for the afterlife.

Price believes that heaven is not a physical place but an image world existing in the minds of the dead. Price puts it this way: "An image-world would have a space all its own. We could not find it anywhere in the space of the physical world."

Price says that it is a world "very much like

Professor H. H. Price described an afterlife similar to a dream. If he is right, our spirits will wander through experience after experience based on our own imaginations and our good or bad actions while alive.

the world of our dreams...There would be [feel images] as well as visual images, [hearing] images and smell images too." This would be a world that was whatever the person imagining it wanted it to be. It would be as limitless as the imagination of the imaginer. For example, a person may wish to hover in a helicopter over a bubble factory in July one minute and wish to be in a submarine floating through a sea of marshmallow créme the next and it would happen. It would happen because that is what the person imagined.

The image-world version of the afterlife works as both heaven and hell. The person who led a good, positive life would have happy memories upon which to base dreams. For example, someone who helped orphans in life would have those rewarding memories to build a spirit world on. On the other hand, someone who was a murderer in life would have feelings of everlasting guilt and shame to contend with in an image world. In this way, the manner in which life is lived determines whether the image world is a paradise or a punishment.

Price's unusual dream-world version of heaven and hell is based on his own interpretations of the experiences of life and death. Most ideas about the afterlife, however, come from many years of religious tradition and belief.

Professor H. H. Price, philosopher and psychical researcher.

Two Common Threads

It is clear that ideas about paradise and punishment change over time and between groups. The medieval European view of the afterlife is different than the modern European view of the afterlife. Heaven to a Jewish person is different than heaven to a Mormon.

There are two similarities between all these heavens and hells. The first thing is that they represent an ultimate destination. The specific ideas about that destination tell a lot about the people who believe in it. Family is important to Mormons, and accordingly heaven is a place where family ties are important; in fact, heaven is run by a Father and a Mother. Throughout history, the Jewish people have been threatened with destruction by other groups. To a Jewish person hell is annihilation, nonexistence, destruction.

The second thing all these different theories have in common is a basis in physical reality. To a large extent, the Mormon heaven is based on an earth-like family with which we are all familiar. H. H. Price compares heaven to a dream and hell to a nightmare. Everyone has experienced a dream and a nightmare. Since no one really knows what happens after death, these reality-based ideas of heaven and hell help make the afterlife less mysterious.

Arguments Against Heaven and Hell

Not everyone agrees with these ideas about the afterlife. David Hume was a British philosopher in the eighteenth century. In studying human behavior, ethics, and morals, Hume arrived at certain conclusions about the nature of heaven and hell. He believed that the spirit died with the body, that there was no afterlife.

One argument that Hume used is that the body and the spirit, or mind, are closely linked throughout life. For example, said Hume, a baby's mind and body are equally unformed. An adult's body is generally as good as it will ever be and the same can be said of that adult's mind. In old age, the body declines and senility sets into the mind. Even when a person is sick his or her mind does not work as well as when he or she is healthy. So, says Hume, the body and the mind are closely linked all through life. It is very strange, then, to

David Hume, eighteenth-century British philosopher, believed most ideas about heaven and hell were nonsense.

say that they are suddenly free of each other at the death of the body. He believed that it is much more logical to conclude that when the body dies the mind dies too.

Hume had another objection to the traditional concept of heaven and hell. Heaven is always viewed as a place where good people go in reward for being good. Hell is a place where bad people are punished for being bad.

Hume pointed out that most people are not all good or all bad. He says, "No one is so utterly good...to deserve...instant translation to a life of eternal bliss;...equally, no one is so wholly bad as to merit nothing but endless torment." People are a combination of good and evil, but the reward and punishment concept treats people as though they are all one or the other. Hume said that an eternity of suffering is a disproportionate punishment even for a very bad person, because that person's crimes were temporary. Even if the person committed crimes almost all his or her life, the crimes would in no way justify an eternity of suffering.

This in turn raises the question whether the idea of hell is consistent with the rest of Christian

One of Hume's objections to ideas about an afterlife relates to the mind-body connection. He said that throughout life, body and mind are closely tied together: In infancy, both are undeveloped; in adulthood, both are at the height of their powers; in old age, both begin to falter. With such a strong connection between the two, he asked, how could it be possible that they would be separated—one dead, one living—after death?

Hume believed that Christian ideas of the afterlife, with absolute reward (heaven) and punishment (hell), were in conflict with Christian philosophy. He pointed out that Jesus Christ was known for forgiveness. Would God, then, be less merciful?

doctrine. Jesus of Nazareth was radical in his day because he taught the need to show unlimited forgiveness to sinners. With this in mind Hume said, "It would be strange indeed to suppose that a message of everlasting torture was an integral part of Jesus' thought."

A comparison would be the treatment of Rudolph Hess, a Nazi official in Hitler's Germany. He was sent to prison for his war crimes. He served more than thirty years. Then, according to Hume, society said, "Enough is enough; no purpose is served in continuing to incarcerate that frail old man for his crimes committed so long ago."

Hume continues: "No matter how dreadful the offense, a time will come when parole is considered and eventually release [be] granted. Is God less merciful than we?" Could the so-called God of Love be more harsh than a parole board? Hume suggested that if the idea of hell is inconsistent with Christian thought, then we must re-examine the idea of heaven as well.

Others who object to an afterlife theory of heaven and hell believe that an eternity of paradise would become boring and thus would be no reward. Most ideas about heaven suggest that every task would be easy and everyone would be perfect. Would life in such a place be dull?

This is a question asked by John Hick, who has written many books on the nature of heaven. He asks where the challenge would be in "a society of perfected individuals in a totally stress-free environment from which pain, sorrow, and death have been banished." It is worth thinking about. Everybody wants things to go smoothly, but it might be boring if you knew exactly what to expect from life for the rest of eternity, even if it was pleasant.

Even heaven as an image world of imagination could eventually run dry. After all, imagination is limited but eternity is limitless.

Science vs. Tradition

Some scientists voice another objection to the theory of heaven and hell. Much of the belief about heaven is based on Scripture, ancient holy

Some people suspect that heaven, a place where souls would be surrounded by nothing but peace and perfection, would be boring.

Do people go to heaven and hell when they die? This
woodcut by fifteenth-century German artist Albrecht Dürer
shows some of the events that the Bible's book of the
Apocalypse says will occur on the day of the Last
Judgment.

writings like the Bible. Scientists question many biblical concepts, such as the creation of the universe and the creation of the human race. Genesis is the first book of the Bible and in it we find a theory for the structure of the universe. It has four main elements. First, God created the earth at the center of the universe. Second, God created the earth specifically for humans. Third, God suddenly created the human race, in the form of Adam and Eve. Fourth, God will keep humans alive after their bodies die, either in heaven or in hell.

Today's scientific knowledge challenges some of these assumptions. The earth is not the center of the universe. It is only one planet of many revolving around the sun. And the sun is only one star of billions in our galaxy and is nowhere near the center of it. Even the galaxy is only one galaxy of one hundred million or so. The earth is definitely not the center of the universe.

There is also very strong evidence to support the idea that human beings were not created suddenly, but evolved slowly over time. The dramatic changes from the earliest pre-humans and early humans to the humans of today were gradual and took place over thousands of years.

Scientific thought has certainly undermined the traditional, literal biblical view of how the earth was formed and how human beings came to live on it. Thus some scientists say that the ideas of heaven and hell must be re-examined closely.

One life leading to a destination of either heaven or hell is not the only theory of the hereafter. Some people feel that humans have many lives and that when people die they come back to live another life on earth. People who believe this are called reincarnationists.

"God will be there in person and we'll see him face-to-face."

Author Hal Lindsey

"One hopes for an opening to another life in which all one's unfulfilled aspirations are realized.... [It is] a form of wish fulfillment."

Paul Kurtz,
In Defense of Secular Humanism

Four

Are People Reborn into New Lives?

Opposite: Many people believe that when we die, our spirit leaves our body and goes on to another life.

Many people believe that the cycle of birth, life, and death repeats. In other words, the death of the physical body leads to rebirth of the spirit into another body. Webster's dictionary defines *reincarnation* as "rebirth of the soul in another body, as in the Hindu religious belief." Reincarnationists believe that instead of going to some spiritual realm, people come back to another earthly life.

The dictionary specified the Hindu religion as a reincarnationist religion. However, many people around the world believe that individual human spirits live in a series of physical bodies. In fact, a 1982 Gallup poll showed that 23 percent of Americans believe in reincarnation.

There are many variations in the beliefs concerning the rebirth of the soul. However, the idea of reincarnation has been most fully developed in the Hindu religion. And most reincarnationists believe at least some of the same things the Hindus believe.

Originating in India, Hinduism is the oldest existing religion in the world. To understand why

"Death is at once final and unique. There is no question of reincarnation."

Theology professor
Father Richard McBrien

"As a man casts off his worn-out clothes and takes on other new ones, so does the embodied self cast off its worn-out bodies and enter new ones."

Hindu holy book *Bhagavad Gita*

reincarnation makes sense to so many people, one must first understand some of the ideas behind this ancient religion.

One important Hindu concept is *karma*. Karma is the idea that what is done in this lifetime determines what the next lifetime will be like. It is as though each person gets plus or minus points for good and bad behavior over the course of a lifetime. The overall behavior in life determines whether the next life, or *incarnation*, is better or worse than the present one. A good life yields a good next life. A bad life leads to an unpleasant next incarnation. Karma is a law but not a lawgiver. In other words, karma is more like the law of gravity than it is like a god. It is not a person. It just is. Someone who is in an unpleasant incarnation is not being punished by a supreme being. That person is suffering the consequences brought about by his or her own actions in a previous life.

Hindus believe that there is a spirit in every person that remains constant throughout the many incarnations. This spirit moves through many bodies and many lifetimes. Just as you will be at age fifty the same person you were at age five, so are people the same in different bodies. This constant spirit is called the *jiva* or soul by the Hindus.

Hindus believe that the concepts of karma and reincarnation answer a question that Jewish and Christian beliefs cannot. They explain why some people are born into better situations than others. One baby is born into a happy and wealthy family; another is born into an angry and poor family. The Hindu explains this apparent injustice by assuming that the first baby led a good previous life and the second baby led a wicked previous life.

The Spirit and the Body

The Hindus believe that our spirits originally

Like Hindus, Buddhists believe in a continuing cycle of
rebirths until a soul is ready to be released from this
cycle and become one with the Great Spirit, Brahma.
This picture shows a Tibetan Buddhist view of the
cycle of rebirths.

If reincarnation is a fact, why are some people born into poor families and others into rich ones? Most believers in reincarnation say that a person is reborn into the life that will teach him or her valuable lessons on the way to achieving Nirvana, or oneness with Brahma.

came from *Brahma*, which roughly means "Everything." There is no English word for this idea. It is a little like the idea of God.

Brahma is bigger than the entire universe. All spirits have come from Brahma. But a long time ago all human spirits were somehow separated from Brahma into physical bodies. This division into the physical body is temporary, and all spirits are constantly moving to reunite with Brahma.

Brahma is something like a chocolate cake and all human spirits are like individual ingredients of the cake. Eggs, milk, sugar, and chocolate are easy to distinguish when they are separate. But when they are mixed together and baked they become part of a much larger whole, and one cannot see them individually anymore. The goal over many lifetimes is to become part of the cosmic cake.

However, the physical body is concerned only

with physical things and those physical things keep people from returning to Brahma. According to Hindu doctrine, the behavior that will bring people closer to Brahma is spiritual.

The conflict between the spiritual and the physical is the state in which all people find themselves from day to day. The spiritual and the physical are opposites that interact with each other all the time. There is no one on earth who is completely spiritual or totally physical. But as a person becomes more spiritual, his or her future lives become closer to Brahma. Eventually the person will be able to break out of the continuous rebirths and rejoin Brahma. This state is called *nirvana*.

This is an oversimplified version of Hinduism. But it is sufficient for the purpose of understanding the Hindu attitudes towards reincarnation.

Ian Stevenson is a college professor who has

A Hindu depiction of Brahma.

spent many years traveling all over the world to investigate reincarnation stories. One of the stories of possible reincarnation that he discovered is about a child who began to speak at an early age about a previous life. Stevenson spoke with many people to verify the story told by the child.

The Story of Bishen Chand Kapoor

Bishen Chand Kapoor was born in India in 1921. His father was a poor railway clerk and his mother was a homemaker. Though the family lived in a small village called Bareilley, two-year-old Bishen was frequently heard to say "Philibhit." Philibhit is the name of a town fifty kilometers away.

As he grew older and learned to speak more, Bishen began to tell of a previous life. Because many people in India believe in reincarnation, his parents and other adults listened to what Bishen had to say and took him seriously.

When Bishen was four years old, his father and brother took him on a train ride to a town some distance past Philibhit. When the conductor announced the Philibhit station, Bishen cried and demanded to get off the train, saying that he "used to live there."

Eventually, Bishen's father spoke with a man who was investigating reincarnation stories. The person, K. K. N. Sahay, asked Bishen a series of questions and then went to Philibhit to investigate.

There he learned of a man named Laxmi Narain who had died just before Bishen was born. He had lived much like the descriptions Bishen gave of his previous life.

Unlike Bishen, Laxmi had been very wealthy when alive. Laxmi had not worked. He had enjoyed drinking and the company of female dancers. He had been very generous. He once

Dr. Ian Stevenson has done extensive research into reincarnation. He has collected case studies of many people from different cultures who may have been reincarnated.

gave a stranger a large sum of money so that person would be able to open a watch dealership.

Laxmi had had a quick temper. K. K. N. Sahay learned that Laxmi had killed a man out of jealousy. Because Laxmi's family had been rich and powerful, Laxmi was not put in jail or punished by the authorities in any way.

Bishen's father and K. K. N. Sahay took Bishen to Laxmi's home, abandoned since Laxmi's death. The house had decayed quite a bit in that time. Bishen was nonetheless able to correctly identify which area had been for men and which for women. Being in Laxmi's house seemed to bring many memories to Bishen about his previous life as Laxmi. For example, he remembered watching female dancers in Laxmi's home. He remembered that he had had a girlfriend, Padma, and a male friend, Sunder Lal. These memories turned out to be accurate. He

Bishen Chand Kapoor, a young Indian boy from a poor family, claimed to have been Laxmi Narain, a rich man, in a previous life.

remembered very specific things too. When asked to describe Laxmi's bed, Bishen was able to describe it down to the correct number and placement of the four pillows.

When Laxmi was a child the family's pickles had become rotten and there were worms in the jars. Laxmi's mother had thrown out the worms but saved the pickles. When she tried to give one to Laxmi, he threw it away in disgust. Laxmi's mother asked Bishen about this incident. "Did you throw away my pickle?" "I did throw away the pickle," Bishen replied, "but...you wanted me to eat worms and [since I did not want to] I threw the pickle away." This response and others convinced Laxmi's mother that Bishen was her son reincarnated.

Finally, there was a story that Laxmi's father had hidden some money. No one had been able to find this money. Laxmi's mother asked Bishen where the money was and he led her and K. K. N. Sahay to a particular room in the house. Bishen was not able to locate the money exactly, but the

Left: Bishen knew the answer when Laxmi's mother asked him about a rotten pickle. Right: Bishen was able to bring Laxmi's family close to the secret spot where Laxmi's father had hidden money.

money was located in that room when it was searched again.

Bishen's story is consistent with the ideas of reincarnation and of karma. Laxmi's own mother and many other people were convinced that Bishen was Laxmi reincarnated.

Remember that Laxmi had killed a man and escaped unpunished? The law of karma says that Laxmi had punished himself by being reborn as a poor clerk's son. Later in life, Bishen was very sorry that he had killed someone as Laxmi. Bishen also regretted being poor.

Ian Stevenson discovered another reincarnation story, this time in South America.

The Story of Marta Lorenz

Maria de Oliveiro was born about 1890 on a large and prosperous ranch in Brazil, South America. She was known to most people as Sinha. She often felt lonely and isolated on her father's ranch. She would travel to the nearby village of Dom Feliciano to visit her friend, Ida Lorenz. Ida was married and had a daughter named Lola. Sinha was very fond of Lola.

Eventually, Sinha fell in love, but the man she loved committed suicide. Sinha became extremely depressed. She intentionally neglected her health. She eventually got sick and was diagnosed as having tuberculosis. In South America at that time, tuberculosis was a deadly disease. Sinha became very ill.

As she lay dying, she told her friend Ida that she had tried to get sick because she wanted to die. She then promised Ida that she would return as Ida's daughter. Sinha predicted that "when reborn and at an age when I can speak...I shall relate many things of my present life, and [that way] you will recognize the truth." She died the next day. This happened in October 1917.

Ten months later Ida Lorenz gave birth to a

"We each have positive traits and talents as well as detrimental habit patterns and attitudes which have been developed in past lifetimes."

Parapsychologist
Florence Wagner-McClain

"None of the accounts... of a recollection of a previous life could be verified."

Catholic theologian Hans Küng

When Sinha de Oliveiro was dying, she told Ida Lorenz she, Sinha, would come back in her next life as Ida's daughter.

baby girl and named her Marta. Ida's other daughter, Lola, the one Sinha had been so fond of, knew nothing of Sinha's promise to return.

When Marta was two and a half years old, she and Lola were returning from a stream after washing clothes there. Marta asked Lola to carry her.

"You can walk well enough," said Lola. "I don't need to carry you."

Marta replied, "When I was big and you were small, I used to carry you often."

Lola laughed and asked Marta when she had been "big." Marta answered, "At that time I did not live here; I lived far from here where there were many cows, oxen, and oranges, and there were also sheep." That described Sinha's farm. As Bishen did in the previous story, Marta described many details of her former life that she would ordinarily have no way of knowing.

Marta also behaved much like Sinha, according to people who knew both of them. Remember

Sinha and Marta had many things in common. Is it possible that Marta was a reincarnation of Sinha?

that Sinha had died of tuberculosis, a disease of the lungs. Until Marta was ten she was especially vulnerable to sicknesses of the lungs. None of Marta's brothers or sisters had similar problems.

Marta's personality was like Sinha's. Both were fond of cats. Sinha never needed to sew, cook, or do other chores because she was from a wealthy family. Instead she spent her time on music and dancing. Marta did not like sewing and aspired to education, even though her poor family could not afford it. Is it possible that Marta's appreciation of education and disdain for household work were a result of the privileged upbringing of Sinha?

Sinha was afraid of rain and Marta also had a fear of the rain. Also, they both had a fear of blood. Marta was the only one in her family who feared blood. There was a woman who knew Sinha, but did not know of Sinha's supposed rebirth as Marta. This woman saw Marta's reaction to blood and commented that it was similar to the way Sinha reacted when she saw blood.

Many people commented that Sinha and Marta had similar handwriting. They were also similar in physical appearance. Another woman who had known Sinha remarked, "This girl [Marta] looks like Sinha."

Marta, Sinha, and their families and friends were not Hindu. Yet this experience is similar to those of Hindus, like Bishen, who believe that they have been reincarnated.

The Constant and Changing Spirit

This brings up two important points about the Hindu views of how we move from incarnation to incarnation, from physical body to physical body. The first is about the nature of the spirit that moves from life to life. The Hindus believe that the spirit is both constant and always changing. These ideas seem to be opposites of each other but are not.

The spirit is constant. For example, the spirit of Sinha is the same as the spirit of Marta. It is the same spirit in two different bodies. Presumably it was the same spirit in a series of bodies before Sinha. Because Marta is now dead, that same spirit is presently in another body. In this way, the spirit is constant.

On the other hand, the spirit is constantly changing. While it is true that you will be the same person at age fifty that you were at age two, it is

Hindus believe a person's spirit is both constant and always changing.

also true that your attitudes, opinions, and beliefs will have changed a great deal in that same period of time. The experiences of the forty-five years in between will have changed you a great deal, though you are still the same person. In that way, the spirit is continually changing.

A favorite Hindu analogy for reincarnation is that of a candle lighting another candle. The flame is the same, only the candle is different. In this analogy, the flame is equal to the spirit and the candle is the body. While the flame is always there, it changes constantly as it is affected by the breeze.

The second point is about *how* the spirit moves from one body to another. Sinha was very confident that she could reincarnate in the time, place, and situation she chose. Apparently she

Like the flame of a candle lighting another candle, a person's spirit moves from one life to another, according to those who believe in reincarnation.

had control over which body she would get in the next life. Many reincarnationists believe that they will be able to choose their next incarnation. This is not true of Hindu belief, however. In the next story we see another example of someone choosing his own next incarnation.

The Story of William George, Jr.

Ian Stevenson traveled to Alaska to interview members of the Tlingit tribe. This native people also has a history of belief in reincarnation. William George was born in about 1890. Near the end of his life, he told his favorite son and daughter-in-law, "If there is anything to this reincarnation business, I will come back and be your son...and you will recognize me because I will have birthmarks like the ones I now have." William had two unique birthmarks on his left arm.

He also gave this favorite son a gold watch given to him by his mother. William told his son to hold the watch for him and to give it back to

Some people believe birthmarks can be evidence of reincarnation if they are the same on a living person as on a person who formerly lived.

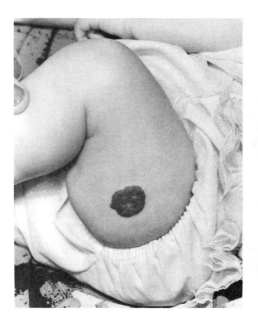

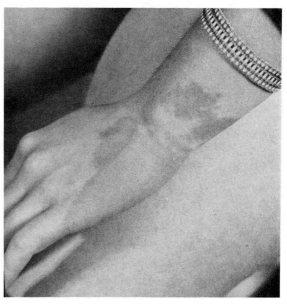

This old German woodcut shows an angel turning the wheel
of life as a soul goes through seven incarnations.

Were William George, Sr., and William George, Jr., the same person in different bodies? Above left, they had similar marks on their bodies, and, above right, the fisherman's grandson had an unusual knowledge of fishing at an early age.

him when he returned as his son's son. William's daughter-in-law, Susan, put the watch in a jewelry box and it stayed there for several years.

Early in August of 1949, William disappeared from his fishing boat. Rescuers searched for his body but it was never found. The waters off the coast of Alaska contain strong currents and are very dangerous.

Shortly after William disappeared, Susan became pregnant with her ninth child. During this pregnancy, she had a dream that William appeared to her and said he was waiting for his grandson.

When her baby boy was born, she and her husband noticed that he had two birthmarks in exactly the same places as William's. They were so impressed by the similarity that they named their child William George, Jr.

As William, Jr., grew, the family noticed many similarities between the boy and his dead grandfather. William, Sr., had injured his ankle severely playing basketball as a young man. He continued to walk with a limp for the rest of his life. William, Jr., also walked with a limp, although he never injured his ankle.

Like Sinha and Marta, the two Williams looked alike. William, Jr., also resembled his grandfather in his habit of fretting and giving advice to his friends and family.

When William, Jr., was four or five years old, his mother opened her jewelry box and removed its contents. William wandered into the room where his mother was and saw the watch given by William, Sr., to his son and daughter-in-law to hold for him. William, Jr., picked up the watch and said "That's my watch." He was very firm in his belief that the watch was his, and he did not want to return it to the jewelry box.

William, Sr., had been a fisherman. William, Jr., showed a strong instinct for the sea and the techniques of fishing. He knew the best bays for catching fish and how to work the nets. He also showed more caution around the sea than did most children his age.

Were the similarities between William George Sr. and Jr. coincidences or evidence of reincarnation?

The story of the two Williams supports the theory of reincarnation. Because of stories like

Virginia Tighe, a Colorado housewife, became known around the world when her hypnotist published a book about her past incarnation as Bridey Murphy, a poor nineteenth-century Irish woman.

these, many people believe in more than one life on earth.

Proving Reincarnation

However, not everyone is convinced. The beliefs of religions such as Christianity, Islam, and Judaism are incompatible with the doctrine of rebirth. Others disbelieve reincarnation because it cannot be proven scientifically. They think that similarities such as those between the two Williams are merely coincidence.

Stories, then, no matter how convincing, are not enough to prove reincarnation. This is because persons claiming to be reincarnated may be able to get information about their "previous life" without having lived it. Information can come from numerous places: films, books, newspaper stories, or conversations overheard on the street. In the book *Who Were You?*, J. Maya Pilkington outlines five things that must be provable beyond a doubt in order to establish reincarnation:

1. That the previous personality did actually exist.
2. That he or she never appeared in books or films.
3. That all details are entirely accurate.
4. That there is absolutely no place where that information could be obtained by the claimant — not newspapers, family, friends, or other places.
5. That no fraud or hoax is intended.

In Marta's case, for example, it is possible that she picked up the details of Sinha's life from her mother, who was Sinha's friend. Perhaps stories of the rich and eccentric Laxmi were told when Bishen was a child, and he learned about Laxmi's life that way. Finally, it is possible that William, Jr., acted like William, Sr., to deliberately mislead Dr. Stevenson into believing that he was his grandfather reincarnated.

Arguments Against Reincarnation

Some examples of reincarnation have been shown to be hoaxes. Sometimes people claim to describe a previous life but instead are telling stories that they have heard or read. The book *Who Were You?* contains a story of a young British woman who was hypnotized. Many people believe that hypnosis is the best way to learn about people's past lives. These people are asked to remember what happened before their birth. What they describe is said to be their past life. In this case, the woman related details of her previous life as Joan Waterhouse, who was tried for witchcraft at Chelmsford, England, in 1566.

Under hypnosis, the young woman repeatedly gave the date at 1556, rather than 1566. A single

These people attended a California reincarnation party. All guests were supposed to come dressed as they looked in a previous life.

mistake like this would not ordinarily have been significant enough to disprove her testimony. But in this case, the same mistake was found on a rare nineteenth-century pamphlet that described the trial in detail.

Because the woman got her information from an inaccurate source, her lie was discovered. There is no way of knowing how many false reincarnation stories go undetected. However, it should be noted that small children like Marta and Bishen would have very little to gain by telling such a lie. Also, these young people would not be very likely to obtain such detailed information without their parents knowing. So, while deliberate hoax may explain some reincarnation stories, all such stories cannot be written off as intentional lies.

William Whalen, a Christian and writer for the magazine *U.S. Catholic*, finds fault with the doctrines of karma and reincarnation. Whalen says that the law of karma is a poor justification for "injustice, suffering, and inequality." According to the law of karma, a person's situation is the result of the actions of a past life. "For example," Whalen writes, "the bad karma accumulated by Adolph Hitler will be inherited by someone else who has no knowledge that he or

Many people believe a person is reincarnated in accordance with the good or bad done in a previous life. A person who lives a good life is reincarnated into a better one; a person who lives a bad life is reincarnated into a worse one. Catholic writer William Whalen believes there would be no point for Adolph Hitler, for example, to be reincarnated into a worse life if the new body could not remember, and learn from, the misdeeds of the previous life.

she was once the Nazi dictator.''

Whalen believes that the law of karma does not serve the function that it is supposed to, allowing a person to learn from and improve from one life to another. Thus, to him, the whole basis of Hinduism does not make sense. He points out that the Bible states emphatically: ''Man is destined to die once, and after that to face judgment'' (Hebrews 9:27).

Where Are Memories Stored?

Some scientists have argued against reincarnation on a biological basis. The argument starts with a question: If I do not remember my previous life, then how can it be said that such a life exists?

People remember things that happen all during their lives. Memories of experiences affect the personality of the individual who experiences them. Memories form the spirit that reincarnationists say moves from body to body.

According to the reincarnationist theory, the spirit is born into the world again and lives another life. Yet when a baby is born, it has no

Those who believe one's spirit is made up of memory, do not think reincarnation is possible because each new life is born with no memory.

What happens when we die? Do we move into a new life?

memories. If these memories are lost at death and cannot be recalled at rebirth, then can it be said that the spirit still exists? Where is it?

Or is it possible that memories are stored in the spirit but are not available for us during our lives? Have you ever forgotten something and remembered it later?

What about *déjà vu*, the feeling that one has experienced something before when the experience is actually a new one. Almost everyone experiences *déjà vu* at some time. Is it possible that this feeling could be a memory, stored away in the spirit?

Is It True?

The theory of reincarnation does not satisfy everyone. Many people are convinced by the incredible accuracy of the stories of Bishen, Marta, and William, Jr. These stories are not final proof of reincarnation, however, because they cannot be proven beyond a doubt.

Many do not believe in reincarnation because it does not seem possible alongside their other religious views. Others believe the stories are either coincidence or outright hoaxes.

Finally, some people do not accept reincarnation because it cannot be proven scientifically. No one, for example, has been able to photograph the spirit and document all the previous lives.

Many have taken this scientific approach to the afterlife question. No one has been able to prove scientifically, beyond doubt, that any kind of life exists after death. For some, this only leads to the conclusion that there is no afterlife at all.

"Many...reincarnation claims can be explained by hidden memories based on the subject's present-life reading and experience."

D. Scott Rogo,
The Search for Yesterday

"Obviously children are too young to have absorbed a great deal of information, especially about deceased people in some distant town."

Reincarnation researcher
Dr. Ian Stevenson

Five

Does Existence End at Death?

When it comes to the immortality of the soul...I can only say that it seems to me to be wholly incredible and preposterous. There is no plausible evidence for it [and] there is a huge mass of irrefutable evidence against it.
H. L. Mencken

Many people would agree with Mencken, an American writer and humorist during the first half of this century. In the twentieth century, more people than ever before believe that the spirit dies along with the body. They believe there is no life after death: no heaven or hell, no reincarnation, no tunnel to go through toward a very bright light.

The growing disbelief in life after death has been brought about largely by two influences. The first is science; the second is a philosophy called *existentialism*.

New scientific knowledge is weakening the foundations of the old religions. For example, the old Christian doctrine included the belief that all human beings descended from two fully developed human beings, Adam and Eve. Today it

Some people believe that when we die we simply
cease to exist; there is no afterlife.

H. L. Mencken thought the idea of an afterlife was ridiculous.

is widely believed that humans evolved through many stages. When parts of a religion's doctrine are shown to be untrue, the rest of its beliefs are called into question.

Science and technology have become very sophisticated. Yet even our most sensitive scientific instruments cannot detect any evidence of life after death.

Existentialism

The second influence, existentialism, is a philosophical movement that stresses existence in the here and now, the freedom of humankind, and the responsibility of each individual for his or her acts. Existentialist ideas have been around for a long time, but the philosophy has matured only in this century. Existentialists generally reject the idea of a spirit outlasting the physical body. A few existentialists do believe in God and the afterlife, but most do not.

The belief that the spirit dies with the body assumes that life is a physical process rather than a spiritual one. In other words, existentialists believe that life amounts to only what can be observed and experienced: birth, life, death, and the decay of the body. Since the spirit is nowhere evident after the death of the body, an existentialist assumes that it no longer exists.

H. L. Mencken speaks of the views towards death expressed by Dr. George W. Crile, a noted surgeon and author of the book *The Phenomena of Life*. Mencken writes, "Crile said that death was acidosis — that it was caused by the failure of the organism [the body] to maintain the alkalinity

When the casket is lowered into the ground, what is left of a person?

Dr. George Crile believed life was a chemical process that ceased to exist when the heart stopped beating.

necessary to its normal functioning." We can see here that the definition of life is not centered on God or the spiritual mission of humankind. It is centered on chemicals. "Life is a struggle," according to Mencken, "not against sin...but against hydrogen atoms." In other words, a human life is not a means to get to heaven or a way to attain a better incarnation the next time around. Life exists for its own sake.

Many people ask, if life completely ends at death, then why do we live? What is life's meaning?

What Is Life About Then?

Existentialists answer in many different ways. Some say that life has no meaning. Milan Kundera, a Czechoslovakian novelist, writes in *The Unbearable Lightness of Being* that "Death has two faces. One is nonbeing; the other is the terrifying material of the corpse." He is saying that all that is left after death is the body, and

This old German woodcut shows death laughing and dancing on a grave. Does death, not life, get the last laugh?

even it eventually will decompose and disintegrate. By "nonbeing," Kundera means that the life that once inhabited the body no longer exists. The implication is that death removes any trace of what once was life. As an essayist in *Time* magazine wrote, death "is a trap door to nothingness." Life, in this case, is like the light from a light bulb. While the bulb is "alive" it provides light, but when the bulb burns out, there is no more light. All that is left is the lifeless shell.

Bertrand Russell did not believe in life after death, but he was not so pessimistic. Russell, born in Britain in 1872, was a philosopher, mathematician, and social reformer. "I believe that when I die I shall rot," he said, "and nothing of my [spirit] will survive." But he did not believe life was meaningless. He wrote: "Happiness is nonetheless true happiness because it will come to an end, nor do thought and love lose their value because they are not everlasting." In other words, it is important to live all you can while you can.

Ancient Egyptian mummies show how well the body can remain preserved. But is that all that is left? Philosopher Bertrand Russell thought so. Still, that did not make life meaningless, he believed. Life is worth living for its own sake.

"The soul is indestructible.... Its activity will continue throughout eternity."

Eighteenth-century German poet Johann Wolfgang von Goethe

"When I am, death is not. When death is, I am not."

Third-century B.C. Greek philosopher Epicuras

The essayist in *Time* magazine asks and answers this question: "Why stay alive in a meaningless universe? The existentialist replies that [people] must live for the sake of living."

Other Ways the Spirit Can Continue After Death

Even if the spirit does not outlive the body, there are other ways it can continue to "live." For example, genetically each child is a combination of chromosomes from both mother and father. Even when a parent dies, part of him or her is alive in the child in a very real way. That part of the parent will continue in the child's children and grandchildren.

A person also lives on in works and deeds. If one affects someone else in a significant and positive way, that person will carry the influence for the rest of his or her life. The same can be said of a negative influence.

Finally, there is a way that every living thing continues and contributes to the world after its death. Jean-Paul Sartre, a French existentialist philosopher, said: "To be dead is to be prey for the living." He meant that in a negative way, but it also serves as a way to think about a process in which every living thing participates. That process is called the food chain.

The Food Chain

The food chain is the basis for all life on the planet earth. Everything must get food, and the food chain illustrates how this happens. In his book *Chains, Webs, and Pyramids*, Lawrence Pringle shows how the food chain begins ninety-three million miles away with the sun.

Energy flows from the sun to the earth. Some of the energy, in the form of light, hits the leaves of plants. Plants photosynthesize the energy and turn it into nutrients. Only plants are capable of turning energy from the sun into nutrients.

2

Even those who do not believe in an afterlife believe
that we live on in the memories and the genes of our
descendants.

A Yugoslavian father lives on after death in the memory of his son.

The plants are then eaten by insects or plant-eating animals such as cows. The insects are eaten by other insects or animals. The animals are eaten by other animals or humans.

The nutrients made available by the plants and the sunlight are never lost during any link on the food chain. But while nutrients are never lost, they change their forms. When you eat a dinner, you consume nutrients from a variety of sources and they then become a part of you. Right now, you may have in your body elements that were once part of a dinosaur, an oak tree, or a dragonfly.

When a plant or an animal dies, the nutrients that are a part of it go back into the food chain.

They are consumed by bacteria and fungi known as *decomposers*. These bacteria and fungi are called decomposers because they break down the nutrients of the animal (or human) body so that they can be used by plants. When they are used by plants, they go back into the food chain again.

In that way, nutrients are never lost and all living things participate in the food chain. Humans eat plants and animals during their lifetimes and consume and use the nutrients. When humans die, all the nutrients they have go back into the food chain to be used again.

So whether or not the spirit lives on after the body, the physical body contributes to the continuation of life in the food chain.

What Is the Nature of Post-Life Existence?

Despite the persuasive arguments in favor of life after death, others make persuasive arguments against the idea. Scientists point to a lack of physical evidence. Existentialists say that the idea of an afterlife is merely wishful thinking.

Others see the afterlife as the impressions made on other people during life. Some say that life comes after death in the form of a contribution to the food chain.

"Death, as the psalmist saith, is certain to all. All shall die."

William Shakespeare, *Henry IV, Part II*

"This embodied [soul] is eternally unslayable.... Thou shouldst not mourn."

Hindu holy book *Bhagavad Gita*

Six

Who Is Right?

Does the spirit live after the death of the body? Does personality survive? Will the meaning and purpose of life become clear after it is all over?

The greatest testimony to the difficulty of these questions is the fact that they have been asked for thousands of years. Hindus and Tlingit Indians believe that the spirit is reborn into another body. Muslims, Jews, and Christians believe that the spirit moves on to an eternal heaven or hell. Though scientists and existentialists give many reasons not to believe in an afterlife, Dr. Moody's interviews with people who have had near-death experiences are too intriguing to ignore.

Will we ever know for certain what the afterlife is like, or even if there is an afterlife at all? Scientists and philosophers — and the rest of us — continue to search for the answer to the question of what happens to us after we die.

Opposite: What happens to us after we die? Although people continue to seek answers, the mystery of death and its aftermath lives on.

Books for Further Reading

Colleen McDannell and Bernhard Lang,
   Heaven: A History. New Haven, CT: Yale
   University Press, 1988.

Raymond Moody, *Life After Life*. New York:
   Bantam, 1981.

J. Maya Pilkington and The Diagram Group,
   Who Were You? New York: Ballantine, 1988.

Lawrence Pringle, *Chains, Webs, and Pyramids*.
   New York: Thomas Y. Crowell Co., 1975.

D. S. Roberts, *Islam: A Concise Introduction*.
   San Francisco: Harper and Row, 1982.

Ian Stevenson, *Twenty Cases Suggestive of
   Reincarnation*. Charlottesville, VA: University
   Press of Virginia, 1966.

Additional Works Consulted

Paul Badham, *Christian Beliefs About Life After Death*. New York: Macmillan, 1976.

The Bible

E. A. W. Budge, *Egyptian Ideas of the Future Life*. London: Kegan Paul, Trench, Trubner, and Co., 1899.

Ellen R. Emerson, *Indian Myths*. Minneapolis: Ross and Haines, 1965.

John Hick, *Death and Eternal Life*. New York: Harper and Row, 1980.

Christmas Humphries, *Karma and Rebirth*. London: John Murray, 1943.

Lex Hixon, *Heart of the Koran*. Wheaton, IL: Theosophical Publishing House, 1988.

David Hume, *Hume on Religion*. New York: Meridian Books, 1963.

Milan Kundera, *The Art of the Novel*. New York: Grove Press, 1988.

Hans Küng, *Eternal Life?* New York: Doubleday, 1985.

H. D. Lewis, *Self and Immortality*. New York: Macmillan, 1973.

H. L. Mencken, *A Mencken Chrestomathy*. New York: Random House, 1982.

Kenneth Ring, *Life at Death*. Quill, NY: Morrow, 1982.

Bertrand Russell, "What I Believe," quoted in *The Encyclopedia of Philosophy*. New York: Macmillan, 1967.

J. R. Smythies, *Brain and Mind*. London: Routledge and Kegan Paul, 1968.

Ian Stevenson, *Cases of the Reincarnation Type*. Charlottesville, VA: University Press of Virginia, 1975.

Essay, *Time*, November 12, 1965.

"I Was Beheaded in the 1700s," *Time*, September 10, 1984.

William J. Whalen, "Reincarnation: Why Some People Expect to Make a Comeback," *U.S. Catholic*, August 1988.

Index

Picture Credits

About the Author

Twenty-four-year-old Tom Schouweiler is a freelance writer who was raised in Marine on St. Croix, Minnesota. He studied English language and literature at the University of Minnesota.

Having lost his father at age eighteen, Schouweiler has naturally considered the question of life after death quite a bit. He believes that it is often the search for the answers to such questions, rather than the answers themselves, that contains the greatest reward.